T0307131

farther

FARTHER

FARTHER

Susan Thackrey

chax
2023

Copyright © 2023 Susan Thackrey
All Rights Reserved

ISBN 978-1-946104-44-1

Library of Congress
Control Number 2023937375

Chax Press
1517 N Wilmot Rd n. 264
Tucson Arizona 85712-4410

Chax Press books are supported
in part by individual donors and
by sales of the books. Please visit
https://chax.org/membership-support/
if you would like to contribute to
our mission to make an impact on
literature and culture in our time.

πολλὰ δ᾽ ὅ γ᾽ ἐν πόντῳ πάθεν ἄλγεα ὃν κατὰ θυμόν

many pains he suffered in his heart upon the sea

Homer, The*Odyssey*

It is in the movement of the particles of meaning
before ideas that our ratios arise.

Robert Duncan, *Bending the Bow*

farther

farther

I

Orders

orders

1.

Argo

punishment wide
as a life some
stellar virulence
propounded day
by day
keelhauled and
shell by shell
undertow prevails
set sail
fifty companions brave and boisterous
fare in disgrace bereaved
of light surveilled
of fifty stories shunned
by dark a
sundering a
surface

orders

2.

Pequot

across the face of
some world
surface mars
original sea
put a face on it
unbearable autopsy
as (no) sinews string
the false anatomy
no gut uncoils to serpent
edible flesh
unfit for consumption
slice of life in
eden eating was all
uncreatured
cannibal
make light of flesh

orders

3.

Nave

premised in place

of promise

corpse in the copse

some trees, a wood

mystery lightens

shred of evidence burden

of proof

of body

hangs

in the balance

broken beam

restored by

force fell on

hard times star-

crossed

orders

"approach the bench with cau-
tion"
judgment is not justice given
exhibits "A" and "B"

orders

4.

mineral planet

important portions of green

mecanique celeste

running in place

impatient placements of green

granite metamorph

no need for

that hypothesis

extremely precarious

event

orders

5.

light is what is

burned

as star as flesh

goes

out hunting bow and

arrow in

the center of

the splintered

  wood a-hunting go

incurring flame

eyes enrolled toward

it is

necessary this

takes place only

world entropical

striking similarity

end vision like

(»)

orders

end game

bird in burning flight

thousand tongues of

tropics veers toward

version

of crux of crucible

   if other need than hunger

   if other sun than fire

   she said

   would be

   a lucidation, a material

   fuel fitting flame

farther

II

Disorders

disorders

1.

what order Milton

mourned for world

arranged in prior

dream singular

demanding grief

opening presumption fruit

past its prime salacious

flesh most sumptuous

before

precoursing multiplicity

   some words there are too subtle to be fixed

   some words there are which I

   cannot explain

disorders

2.

point of order
same time illusion
light constant now
superluminal speed
of propagation she
permitted herself
to be
admired blood
streaming from the accident
of substance
canal running
to sea
incarnadine over
time
getting over
it forgot word incarnadine
blasphemous as
painting sun red

disorders

3.

over broken

heart of red

riding hood child hood

not allowed to see who

got it

before now

forgets it

hooped ruse

circumscribe circular

binding breath

taking expanse as

authority punctual

it is in

time parsing

pin points

still the angel of

the line of demarcation

disorders

4.

succumbed to

womb mother

peeled from

us no

end in sight

what remains

as rind

mind games

gambling innocence

of invention noon

striking light

and the speed of light

to which we have

adapted time and

time again

twisting wisdom

"context or oblivion"

disorders

5.

meridian of fire

crossing recrossing

inscribing what it

makes

blue as

beautiful blue

domed inner

skull of

sky igniting

suffering

as day

disorders

6.

lightning lit

not

at hazard

but bolt

brilliant flesh

of accurate

generation

world

rose

rested

from matter

beyond

apocalypse

farther

III

Against Orders

against
orders

1.

in order to

the only mistake was
starting at the beginning
a shade, a sheaf, a ledge
each error in its
own right
star mapping source
until eye
slipped bleeding
stars a
strophe, a stroke
red shift moving
too fast to notice
juxtaposition inducing
relativity golden grave
of pure necessity
un coup de grace

(»)

against
orders

un coup de des

a whole

new world ruled

in tiny lines curving so

beautifully seen from another

sphere mere horizon

in blood shot

eye unowned

precursor

toolmaker repeater

a strophe a stroke

as revelation runs

amok serving

two masters

it is "entirely

composed of

embryonic

lunar light"

against
orders

2.

digesting chance
and fate
alike
inextricable mercy em-
bedded in
time to whom does
time belong before
prediction after
fear even in the
presence of wonders
something stays the
water is also the
movement in the
water
its etymology it
has no etymology

against
orders

3.

assault assail modulating

backward toward

assay help

angels make

hay in the shining

the corrupting

beady-eyed gleaners

sharp-tongued scavengers

spoilage corvid

crows ravenous

picking it

out last

taboo of

skin and bark the red

robe of Beatrice her

before picture the

world's clothing

(»)

against orders

wholly sensation

the woman clothed in the

sun bundle

bound in

solar circuit golden

baled an

instance

against

orders

4.

desire developing

what passes for

carrying thought out

passing out past

shroud shield war

will all that

would whip into

shape won at

greatest odds

historical surrounds

shattered source

accounting for our

archaeology old

logos parsing out

collage of disaster

laying out in

lines bodies body

parts shards shells

(»)

against
orders

partly broken

common ancestor

bones of Lucifer

now lucy in

oldevai gorge one

tooth called

denisovan for

purposes of

identification infinite

regressing of definition

   calculus of envy

   calculus of splinter

   calculus of spleen

against orders

5.

who knew

our living was

our dying every

door doubling

entry into

leaving rhyming

rehearsal shading

grieving into

greeting pacing

pacing in the dim

galactic

room believing

itself magical

he said

there is

no reporting of

suffering there is no

legitimate imagining of

(»)

against
orders

suffering pasting

stars into

pattern perceiving

limit perishing end

in dark end in

excess of light

for Wes Taft

against
orders

6.

Einstein's Grammar

traveling to Singapore
I do not
bring Singapore into
existence or in travelling
to Singapore I do
bring it into
existence the city
is there and
in travelling towards
me it does or doesn't bring
me into existence at
the same time travelling
toward death I don't
bring death
into existence I reach
death but the

against
orders

city was there all along

mean time

in travelling to

death I do

bring death into

travelling toward me bringing

me into the city

there all along all

along

against
orders

7.

come to this

rubble and

muttering eyes

and ears

undone a

wrack and

snare

littoral meaning "where

it flows"

literal

against
orders

8.

cobble my
hooves the
spark is
both our
tinder path
alight

farther

IV

O rders

orders

1.

unappointed

star begins

night weapon what

might have been

memory a thousand and

one worlds

orders

2.

same old forest

unceasing

animal squabble

short circuit celestial

silent round

capping our

learning with

some

sieve for

sifting toil

of words

> "nothing will come of nothing —
> speak again"

depth charge hoisting

burden of

catechism into tiniest

planetary

orders

fragments raining freshly

down

act of justice

any act of justice

orders

3.

(Odysseus)

wide blue sky

perceiving

all

that is this

light

shines on

this

place land

that is

no where (now here)

time that divides

itself itself

knowing where

to stop empty

coracle

beyond

(»)

orders

landfall his

heart upon

the sea

upon the _____

orders

4.

tyrannical constructions

how hard as

heart

gerrymandering no

matter into proving

pity into

reproving

providence or

whatever musics or

is

this

infinitely moving

fraction

of illusion

illusion of

ocean

elusion of

ocean

orders

5.

if

I wanted I

could enter

water

where skin

breaking

surface breaking

each named and

willing

reflection thing

shudders with

movement of any

other there

never was pool

so perfectly

unmoved a

Narcissus could

make perfect first

mistake

orders

6.

any

first perception

takes

a likeness

spitting

image

what is

noticed is

not

pure or purely

random even

trying to leave

it alone

or let

it loose noose

tightens

orders

7.

betrayed into

decay of

"as if"

weight of memory

were not

enough leaf

memory tree

memory bird-brain

re-membering 13

million flight

years lent to

soften knowledge

"memento mori"

"the icon of the

brimming bowl"

traced through 100 years

of Netherlandish

(»)

orders

history

outlandish portrayed too

large or too

small some

function of the

telescope of

time

traveler or function of

some end not

in sight

trying to

zero in

orders

8.

derelict links

disintegrate

these

pieces

constant as

space-trash surrounds

our

O

discarded

knowledge time

beyond

form impossibly

broken

orders

9.

crevasse

deepening

between

what is and

O ordering

orbiting darkness as

light some

kind of

brilliance

unsynapsed not

reflecting

cosmos matter

of dark

dark of

energy dissolving

distance to

denseness I

(»)

orders

thought I said re-

solving no matter

blackest whole

panic in phantom

limb is

that limb

it is

losing solid

ground yearning

toward cohering

growing

limb after

limb

trying to absolve

salt taste time

remains grasping

the sea itself

fishing for

creaturehood

(»)

orders

keeping its

eye out

for some

common

rhyme

orders

10.

word at end
as end entering
first image
always compass
encompassing passing
collapsing
as if beauty
were complete not
yet another
path pushing or
is it calling
past
circumference comfort
falling into thin
air ear
finally able
perceiving
taking it
through that
door that

orders

11.

urgent problem

encyclopedic

encircling but

names rain

down into

air mouths

touching thirst

of tongues to

tell names raining

down in

exactitude

of compassion weight

calibrated one

faultless

name drops

exactly onto leaf

letting it fall

(»)

orders

into entity

bare bough now

also entity

you may

in me   behold

orders

12.

in dark

timelight

it works makes

shape of

current

face

flowing whether

or not

in poor

sunlight

bomb-blown we

see or save

or want to

see or save

only

a fool calls

a stone

a thing

orders

13.

horizon lingering

coracle

beyond

land's end

they said the

boat was

rowed at

night by the

hands of stars

her heart

upon

the sea

orders

14.

my vulture

trolling

again

for death

broken

circle

finely spiralled

diminishing arc

upon arc

toward final

flesh and cross-

boned marrow honed

and harrowed opened to

the bluest

air breathing

breath of bird

before I go

breathless

into

breathing earth

V

O

0.

entrust myself unto this dungy earth
and with the ragged boy with purpled mouth
who romps companion to the wretchedest
within this ragged throng, I'll let wind starve
my cheeks sun blind my eyes age decay
each faculty that lets me name myself
as human still alive and burning live
and call myself immortal celestial
sum of suns until the still unnamed
day that self-same ragged boy unmasks
himself and me shattering the
celestial shell blue barrier to heaven

farther

About Susan Thackrey

Susan Thackrey, a poet who lives and works in San Francisco, began to compose poetry at the age of three. She was an inaugurating student in the Poetics Program at New College in San Francisco in 1980, and studied with Robert Duncan and Diane di Prima formally and informally over a number of years. Thackrey has given invitational lectures on Robert Duncan, Charles Olson, and George Oppen, including as a keynote speaker at the George Oppen Conference in Buffalo, and more recently on Duncan's *The H.D. Book* for the San Francisco Poetry Center. Since reading Homer over a five year period with Duncan and some of her poet contemporaries, an important and lively part of her life in poetry has almost always included variously focused and long-lived reading groups with other poets.

Her day jobs have included co-founding and managing the art gallery Thackrey and Robertson in San Francisco, as well as her current work as a Jungian analyst in the C.G. Jung Institute of San Francisco. There she has taught, spoken, and published, focusing especially on art, including publishing a talk and essay on Jung's paintings for *The Red Book: Reflections on C.G. Jung's Liber Novus* (Routledge).

Her poems have appeared in a number of journals, including *Five Fingers, Hambone, Talisman, Traverse,* and *Volt.* Current books in print, in addition to *Farther,* are *Empty Gate* (Listening Chamber), *George Oppen: A Radical Practice* (O Books and The San Francisco Poetry Center), and *Andalusia* (Chax).

farther

About Chax

Founded in 1984 in Tucson, Arizona, Chax has published
more than 240 books in a variety of formats, including
hand printed letterpress books and chapbooks, hybrid
chapbooks, book arts editions, and trade paperback
editions such as the book you are holding. Chax also creates
programs that engage students of literature and of the arts
of the book, through classes and workshops. Chax presents
several public events each year, including poetry readings,
artists' talks, and small symposia on topics of poetics, the
arts, and our social culture.

Your support of our projects as a reader, and as a
benefactor, is much appreciated.

You may find CHAX at *https://chax.org*

farther

Fonts used in this book are Gill
Sans and Albertina Pro.

Designed by Charles Alexander
at Chax Press, and printed by KC
Book Manufacturing.